DEATH VALLEY NATIONAL MONUMENT

A PICTORIAL HISTORY

BY JAMES W. CORNETT

© 1986, 1993 by Death Valley Natural History Association
All rights reserved. Published 1986. Third Edition 1993

ALBION
PUBLISHING GROUP

Albion Publishing Group
924 Anacapa Street, Suite 3A
Santa Barbara, CA 93101
(805) 963-6004

Designed by Gay Hagen
Edited by Janie Freeburg

Printed in Thailand
through Asiaprint Ltd., U.S.A.

ISBN 1-878900-10-2 (previously ISBN 0-917859-19-7)

From top: Mud cracks after a rain; Amargosa River. Wind sculpted ripples at the Sand Dunes. Gnarled trunk of an ancient bristlecone pine. Rock pattern in Mosaic Canyon.

Opposite: Eroded hills near Zabriskie Point.

Preceding page: Death Valley from the Telescope Peak trail.

Acknowledgments

The most important people to acknowledge and thank for the publication of the book are the members of the Death Valley Natural History Association. A special thanks to Mary and Ray Parks, two NHA members who brought us together with Sequoia Communications, and to the Association's Board of Directors for their guidance and contributions.

We also recognize the invaluable contribution of the National Park Service: Ed Rothfuss, Superintendent; Shirley Harding, Librarian/Curator at Furnace Creek; Sue Buchel, Librarian/Curator at Scottys Castle; Naturalist Phil Zichterman; Frank Sumrak; and the entire staff of Death Valley National Monument. These people should be commended for the care and continued preservation of Death Valley.

And to Virgil Olson, Death Valley's Chief Naturalist, now retired after 23 years in the National Park Service (the last nine in Death Valley), whose priceless experience, patient guidance and personal dedication ushered this final product to the Park visitor: "I wish a heartfelt thanks to my mentor and friend."

Jamie Gentry

Jamie Gentry
Business Manager, Death Valley
Natural History Association

Photo Credits

Contents

CHAPTER ONE

The First Gold-seekers

"Before us lay a splendid scene of grand desolation . . ."
William Manly, 1849, upon entering Death Valley for the first time.

Death Valley National Monument captivates us all. Whether one is a casual observer or serious student, the stark desolation and dramatic landscape are without parallel. In times past Death Valley was the home of an ancient people who lived along the shoreline of a prehistoric lake. Today the valley is the driest, hottest spot in North America. At its most fascinating, Death Valley is a lavishly illustrated textbook revealing tremendous forces that uplift rugged mountain peaks and allow the earth to drop to the lowest point in the western hemisphere. It was this desert environment coupled with rugged terrain that wrought unbelievable hardships upon the early pioneers and prospectors who first came to "the valley of death."

For at least 9,000 years Indians knew of the region now called Death Valley. Indeed, they lived between its steep walls and quite possibly hunted mastodons and giant ground sloths, animals far larger than the bighorn sheep that roam the landscape today. But the valley was not a desert then. Rainfall was more plentiful, summer temperatures were not so extreme and huge "Lake Manly" covered the valley floor. Over a period of many thousands of years the northward retreat of glacial ice caps and the migration of most Pacific storm systems to higher latitudes created a desert climate that was to dominate all facets of life here for the next 8,000 years. This was the environment encountered by the first known white people who entered the valley in 1849.

Left: The Zabriskie Hills.

Above: A prospector's lonely grave.

Above right: Rock layers depict Death Valley's geologic history.

Above left: An Indian rock dwelling provided shelter from desert winds.

The harshness of the desert landscape was not fully comprehended by William Manly, John Rogers and the "Jayhawker" party as they headed out west for the California goldfields. Their quest was one of wealth. Gold had been discovered in California and was waiting for those hardy individuals who staked the first claims. The Jayhawkers, like thousands of other easterners that would follow them, were unaccustomed to traveling through desert lands; none were fully prepared for the trials that lay ahead. Nevertheless, on October 1, 1849, the Jayhawkers, along with several other parties heading for California, left the final staging point at Salt Lake City. It is said that the original amalgamation of wagons totaled 107 with over 200 eager gold-seekers aboard.

Two days out of Salt Lake City, the emigrants encountered Captain Wesley Smith leading a California-bound pack train of traders. For unknown reasons, Smith revealed a map to the Jayhawkers purporting to show a cutoff from the Old Spanish Trail that would lead them due west to Walker Pass. Such a shortcut would save weeks on the journey and take them to the goldfields that much sooner. But eighty of the wagon drivers played it safe and decided not to follow Smith's map. This group headed south toward San Bernardino in southern California. The remaining twenty-seven wagons proceeded west toward Death Valley and some of the most rugged terrain in North America.

The group encountered extreme hardships. The twenty-seven wagons managed just fifteen miles a day — a distance now covered by automobile in fifteen minutes! The land offered little food and many of the oxen used to haul the wagons had to be slaughtered for meat. One by one, wagons were left behind and precious belongings sacrificed to the elements. Springs were few; more than once a mother would try to comfort her child who cried out for water. In this condition, the remnants of the Jayhawker party entered a long, narrow valley on Christmas day, 1849.

Just prior to descending to the valley floor a group of bachelors broke ranks and decided they must head north

Above: The Grapevine Mountains.

Left: Prospectors with their ever-present burro companions. The ideal desert pack animal, the burro can survive on little water and sparse vegetation.

Above: Cottontop cactus in the Hells Gate area.

Opposite: An aerial view of Death Valley's sand dunes.

while several families led by William Lewis Manly would continue west. The families were left at a spring near present-day Furnace Creek to rest and await Manly's return from a scouting mission in search of a passage out of the valley. In his absence, Indians killed three oxen in retribution for the group's stealing squashes several days earlier. To add further to their misery, Manly announced upon his return that no western or northern route existed through the rugged Panamint Mountains. They could only head south if they were to have a chance of escaping the valley. A day's travel on foot led them to a source of water later named Bennett's Well.

With only one wagon, almost no food, and faint from exhaustion, the group devised a last desperate plan. The two youngest and most able-bodied men, Manly and Rogers, would leave the group at the camp and venture forth on foot over the mountains to seek food and assistance. The party felt sure that the village of Los Angeles must be just beyond the Panamints and that Manly and Rogers could return in ten days with supplies. No one in the group could have known that Los Angeles was over two hundred miles away. Manly and Rogers would not make it back to Death Valley for over three weeks.

At first Manly and Rogers were no more successful on foot than with wagons. They failed in their initial attempt to penetrate the mountain wall to the west. Eventually, they did find a pass through the Panamints. Later they passed the corpse of a Mr. Fish, one of the bachelors they had parted with days before. He had apparently died of exhaustion after escaping the valley. But Manly and Rogers persisted. After enduring nearly two weeks of thirst and hunger they succeeded in reaching

Newhall, near present-day Los Angeles, in early January. Spanish-speaking ranchers graciously provided them with food and pack animals so they might save their comrades still waiting in the valley.

Over twenty-one days had passed since they had gone for help and Manly and Rogers were fearful of what they might find. When they finally reached the valley they were distressed to discover the body of Captain Culverwell, a member of their party. Was this the fate of everyone? On approaching the lone wagon at Bennett's Well, no sign of life could be seen. Nervously, Manly shot his rifle into the air. As if by magic a man got up from beneath the wagon and upon seeing Manly and Rogers shouted, "The boys have come, the boys have come!"

Only the Bennett and Arcane families were left. The others, such as Captain Culverwell, had struck out on their own when they feared that Manly and Rogers would not return. The fate of some of the others remains unknown to this day. Weak and still frightened at the prospect of a hundred-mile march across the desert to Los Angeles, it is said that one of the women named the place of their suffering when they ascended the last ridge out of the valley. She looked back one last time and said, "Goodbye, Death Valley."

Although three members of the 49'ers perished crossing the desert, only Captain Culverwell actually died within Death Valley proper. Tragically, he would not be the last of its victims. The valley's name would stick as tales of its horrors became immortalized — though often grossly exaggerated — by the press. Historians would later write that "no region of the United States . . . has taken such a legendary toll of life or gained so evil a reputation as Death Valley."

Plants and Wildflowers of Death Valley

arly pioneers described Death Valley as "destitute of all vegetation," but in fact a remarkable diversity of plantlife is found here. Almost 1,000 species occur within the Monument, a list that includes ten ferns, six lilies, and two orchids! Twenty-one flowering plant species are found nowhere else in the world — including the yellow "Panamint daisy," the blue-flowered "Death Valley sage," and the small-blossomed "goldcarpet."

Although most visitors hope to see vast panoramas of spring wildflowers, not every winter brings sufficient rain to make the desert bloom. Above-average amounts of precipitation in November and December are necessary to germinate a profusion of spring annuals. More rains through January and February allow them to continue growth so that a maximum bloom is assured. The first warm days of late February and early March bring rapid development of the stems and buds, followed shortly thereafter by the simultaneous appearance of millions of flowers. Within Death Valley National Monument some of the best displays are in the south end of the valley where primrose, sand-verbena, lupine, and sunflowers grow close to the roadside for easy viewing and picture-taking.

In addition to wildflowers, cacti are common. Although the well-known giant saguaro of the Sonoran Desert is absent here, Death Valley has at least thirteen varieties including calico, old man, cottontop, and golden cholla cactus. Cacti bloom in the spring and produce some of the most beautiful flowers in the plant kingdom. The showy magenta blossoms of the beavertail cactus, one of Death Valley's most abundant species, can be seen from many of the roads which traverse gravelly soils above 1,000 foot elevations.

Desert plants utilize three basic evolutionary strategies to cope with the arid environment in which they live. Ephemeral or *annual* plants lie as dormant seeds throughout most of the year, germinating only after winter rains moisten the soil. They grow rapidly, develop flowers and seeds within a few short weeks, and then die as summer approaches. Creosote, cacti and other perennials *endure* drought conditions by collecting water through specialized root systems. They conserve this water through a variety of means including reduction in leaf size, shedding of leaves entirely, or closing down pores in the leaf surfaces during daylight hours. A final category of plants *evade* arid conditions by growing in places where runoff from storms collects. Arrowweed and salt bushes are most frequent on the valley floor where subsurface moisture collects. Cottonwoods and true willows are common at higher elevations near canyon springs fed by past storms.

Death Valley National Monument is much more than low, hot desert. Incorporated within the monument are lofty mountains such as Telescope, Wildrose, and Grapevine Peaks, all of which rise over 8,000 feet above the valley floor. The low temperatures and high precipitation of the mountain environments support distinctly different plant species, including pinyon, juniper and grizzly bear cactus at intermediate elevations; and limber and ancient bristlecone pines on the mountaintops.

Opposite: Golden Evening Primrose carpets the desert near Jubilee Pass.

Opposite top, from left: Globe mallow; creosote bush; desert five-spot; rock nettle.

Above: A young cottontop cactus.

CHAPTER TWO
The Sights and Faces of the Land

The stark Death Valley landscape reveals all. Rocks and formations that are obscured by vegetation or obliterated by heavy rainfall in less arid regions are laid bare for all to see in this land of fault scarps, volcanoes, and contorted rocks.

Death Valley, unlike many other valleys, was not carved by a river. Rather it is the result of fractures or "faults" in the Earth's brittle crust. Geologists term this kind of valley a fault basin or "graben." In the Death Valley region, movements along faults allowed one portion of the Earth's crust to slip or "down drop" past another. As portions or "blocks" of the crust were down-dropping to create valleys, they were also being tilted or "rotated" to the east. As the eastern edges of the crustal blocks tilted down, the western edges rose up creating mountains. The Panamint Range along the western edge of the Monument and the Amargosa Range along its eastern edge are but two results of the process. Although much of the landscape of eastern California and most of Nevada is composed of this "basin and range" topography, Death Valley is the most dramatic example of the phenomenon.

Geologically speaking, Death Valley is young. The rounding and leveling forces of erosion, at work for only a short time, have left the rugged, precipitous landscape intact. Although the age of our planet is approximately four and one-half billion years, Death Valley was formed in just the last three million years, scarcely a grain of sand in the hour-glass of earth history. Generally speaking, exposed rocks are much

Opposite: Majestic Tin Mountain. Volcanic ash in the foreground, a result of the Ubehebe Crater explosion, is now a habitat for desert holly.

Above: The eroded mudstones of the Furnace Creek Formation, viewed from Zabriskie Point.

Top: Winter on Telescope Peak.

Above: A bristlecone pine.

Opposite: The expanse of cracked mud at the Racetrack is one of Death Valley's unusual features.

Opposite, inset: One of the Racetrack's mysterious "moving rocks." A combination of wind and rain moves heavy rocks over the slick mud playa. Rocks up to 400 pounds have moved this way.

older than the creation of the valley and surrounding mountains. Formations dating back to the Mid-precambrian Period 1.8 billion years ago comprise the sombre grey parts of the Black Mountains and are easily seen as one drives the paved road from Badwater south into Jubilee Pass.

Mountain Ranges Create a Desert

Death Valley is surrounded on all sides by steep-sided mountains. Although the initial uplifting of these mountains began some 8 to 10 million years ago, it is only in the last three million years that they have risen dramatically in elevation. Their relative youth — and the scarcity of precipitation which might otherwise smooth off their sharp edges — makes these mountain slopes rugged and starkly beautiful.

The mountains to the west of Death Valley create a "rain shadow" effect and are essentially responsible for the arid conditions that prevail on the valley floor. Each winter storm traveling east off the Pacific Ocean must rise as it

passes over the ranges in its path. As a storm climbs to higher altitudes, it cools and its capacity to hold moisture decreases, resulting in the condensation of water into droplets. Most of these droplets fall as rain or snow when the storm ascends the western or "windward" slopes of the ranges. By the time the storm clouds reach the valley floor they have been wrung dry of their moisture. Storms coming off the Pacific Ocean must first pass over the Coastal Ranges, then the Sierra Nevada, and then the Argus and Inyo Mountains before reaching the Panamints. In all, there are four rain shadows which must be confronted by eastward traveling storm systems. No wonder Death Valley is the driest place in North America, averaging less than two inches of precipitation per year!

Telescope Peak in the Panamint Range, reaching 11,049 feet above sea level, is the highest point within Death Valley National Monument. Near the summit is a stand of bristlecone pines, a species of tree which occasionally may live to be more than 4,000 years old, placing it among the oldest living things on our planet. Pinyon and limber pines, as well as juniper, can also be found

throughout the high country of the Panamint Range. The Cottonwood Mountains (actually part of the Panamint Range) lie just to the north with their highest point, Tin Mountain, reaching 8,953 feet in elevation.

The mountains forming the eastern wall of Death Valley are not as tall, though certainly as steep, as the Panamints. The Grapevine, Funeral and Black Mountains, running north and south, are collectively known as the Amargosa Range. Grapevine Peak, near Scottys Castle, is the highest point in Death Valley's eastern mountains, reaching an elevation of 8,738 feet. The magnificent Dantes View vista point lies in the Black Mountains of the Amargosa Range.

Dantes View

One of the most photographed vistas within Death Valley National Monument may be seen from Dantes View, situated almost 6,000 feet above the valley floor. The perspective is grand in the extreme, with a view as breathtaking as any in the country. Standing on the western edge of the Black Mountains, one can gaze to the west, view the winter snow on the Panamint Range and easily pick out Telescope Peak rising abruptly above the barren salt flats of the valley floor. Below, strange patterns reveal a fascinating array of salt deposits including gypsum and rock salt that cover more than 200 square miles. Badwater is straight down the mountainside. Large, black ravens often frequent the overlook. Officials of the Pacific Coast Borax Company named the viewpoint; they were said to have been inspired by the description of purgatory in Dante's *Inferno*.

Badwater

The lowest point in the Western Hemisphere lies at Badwater in Death Valley National Monument. At 282 feet below sea level, this spot is testimony to the downward sliding of the valley floor along faults in the Earth's crust. Relatively speaking, the surface here has been dropping faster than the piling up of sand, silt, and gravel washed out from the surrounding mountains.

The small spring-fed pool at Badwater is the only reminder of an ancient lake that covered the floor of Death Valley at intervals during the Pleistocene Ice Age. Called "Lake Manly" by modern geologists, this body of water at one time reached 90 miles in length, six to eleven miles in width and had an estimated depth of nearly 600 feet! Abundant precipitation and cooler temperatures during the past several hundred thousand years resulted in tremendous runoff not only in the surrounding mountains but in the Sierra Nevada mountains fifty miles west of Death Valley National Monument. Ancient rivers draining the eastern slopes of the Sierras had no outlet to the ocean, and flowed inland to the lowest point in the region — Death Valley. With the end of the last ice age and the spread of aridity in southwestern North America over the past 10,000 years, runoff dramatically decreased. Coupled with soaring evaporation rates due to higher temperatures, this resulted in the drying up of ancient "Lake Manly" and the creation of a huge salt playa in its place.

Although the pool at Badwater is salty, plant and animal life is not absent. Wiggling soldier fly larvae abound and bronze water beetles can be seen searching for algae. Patches of ditch grass grow in clumps near shore and the salt-tolerant pickleweed is found at the water's edge.

Opposite, top: Death Valley from Dantes View.

Opposite, below: The salty, spring-fed pool at Badwater.

Above: A raven at Dantes View.

Sand Dunes

Opposite, above: Death Valley's sand dunes.

Below, from left: A kit fox rests from a night's hunt for rodents; sidewinder tracks; a banded gecko, found in all parts of Death Valley; raven tracks in the sand dunes.

Deserts are popularly thought of as vast regions of sand dunes. In fact, Death Valley is typical of desert environments throughout the world: It is covered with less than 5% windblown sand. What is special about sand dunes is that they present an entirely different appearance to the normally harsh desert landscape and provide a unique habitat for desert plants and animals. Dunes appear soft, inviting and — in the low light conditions of early morning and late afternoon — almost seem to be illuminated from within. Sand dunes are also dynamic. With every major windstorm individual grains are transported and redeposited, thus altering both the shape and position of many of the dunes.

The most conspicuous dunes in Death Valley National Monument are confined to an area of about fifteen square miles near Stovepipe Wells Village. The sand is a product of erosion from the Cottonwood Mountains to the west and northwest. A close examination of the grains of sand reveals both light and dark fragments. Black grains are generally a combination of iron and oxygen known as magnetite; most white grains are quartz.

An early morning or late afternoon visit to the dunes reveals one of the more intriguing aspects of their appearance — evenly spaced ripples. These are tiny piles of heavy sand grains that accumulate at a perpendicular angle to the wind. Simply explained, winds of varying velocities sort out different sized grains with the larger grains lagging behind, forming long ridges.

Dune fields have their own unique assemblage of plants and animals. Fiddleneck, woolly marigold, and certain varieties of locoweed are often associated with dune systems. The sidewinder rattlesnake, desert kangaroo rat *(Dipodomys deserti),* and kit fox appear to reach their greatest abundance

Above: An alluvial fan, near Tucki Mountain.

Opposite: Devils Golf Course.

Inset: Snow-like salt crystals, found on the Valley floor.

in areas of loose, windblown sand. A walk out onto the dunes in the early morning often reveals animal tracks indicating those species that were active the night before.

Alluvial Fans

At the mouth of most canyons emptying into Death Valley are deposits of sand and gravel (alluvium) washed down from the surrounding mountains during unusually heavy rains and subsequent runoff. From a distance, these sloping deposits appear fan-shaped, hence the name alluvial fan. Although they may be obscured in other environments, the lack of vegetation in Death Valley makes these deposits readily observable here.

Death Valley's largest alluvial fans lie at the mouths of east-facing canyons along the base of the Panamint mountains. A second spectacular group of fans rise from the salt pan to canyons in the Funeral Range along the east side of the valley.

Devils Golf Course

The unbelievably rugged surface in the center of Death Valley is aptly named Devils Golf Course. Its jagged pinnacles are rock-hard salt crystals composed mostly of table salt (sodium chloride) with some silt mixed in. The salt layer is about three feet thick and rests on a bed of mud which underlies much of the valley. The salt pinnacles were originally formed by capillary action when a shallow lake disappeared due to increasing aridity about two thousand years ago. As the water evaporated away, salt precipitated out as crystals, many of them forming sharp ridges and peaks. Occasional rains keep them sharp. Some reach nearly two feet in height and can cut through leather.

Ubehebe Crater

About 4,000 years ago, a tremendous explosion occurred in Death Valley, undoubtedly one heard and felt by the Indian inhabitants of the time. Not far from the present day location of Scottys Castle, a rising plume of molten basalt came in contact with the overlying watertable. The water instantaneously flashed to steam, creating an explosive pressure that knocked off the mantle of sedimentary rock above and blew a crater in the ground one-half mile across and 500 feet deep. The crater would become known in Panamint Indian legends as "the basket in the ground."

Today, this evidence of volcanic activity is called Ubehebe Crater. There are actually more than a dozen explosion craters in the area; Ubehebe is the largest and most recently created. No lava flows occurred at the site but volcanic cinders and ash, in some places 150 feet thick, covered the ground from two to five miles in every direction.

Zabriskie Point

One of the most colorful and dramatic vistas in Death Valley National Monument can be found at Zabriskie Point. The yellow mud hills surrounding the view point, uplifted within the last few million years, are ancient lakebed sediments of the Pliocene Furnace Creek Formation that predate Lake Manly. The fine-grained muds and siltstone that comprise the hills prevent absorption of very much water: most runs off. Such surface run-off results in deep furrowing of the

Above left, Ubehebe Crater — one-half mile across, 500 feet deep, the result of a steam explosion.

Left: Layers of uplifted, tipped sediment formed Striped Butte in the South West part of Death Valley National Monument.

landscape, creating badlands that support almost no vegetation. To the west can be seen the salt beds on the valley floor and the towering Panamint Mountains whose summits mark the western boundary of Death Valley National Monument. The point is named for the late Christian Brevoort Zabriskie, a onetime vice-president and general manager of the Pacific Coast Borax operations in Death Valley.

Artists Palette

J ust nine miles south of the Visitor Center lies the turnoff for Artists Drive, a paved, nine-mile driving excursion through one of the most colorful parts of Death Valley National Monument. The road lies atop steep alluvial fans, winds through washes, and passes through canyons bounded by mudhills. It climbs steadily above the valley floor, offering a sweeping view back across the salt flats. Multi-colored hills, representing 5,000-foot thick deposits of cemented gravels, ancient lake sediments and volcanic debris, here form the front of the Black Mountains. The rocks of the Artists Drive Formation have yielded diatoms and microscopic plants indicative of an environment which existed some ten to thirty million years ago. The composition of rock pigments at Artists Drive is, to a certain extent, unknown. However, iron oxides are thought to be responsible for the reds, yellows, browns, blacks and other intermediate shades. Purple hues are due to magnesium. Although copper is often responsible for the green color of rocks, some geologists believe the greens of the Artist Drive Formation are the result of the breakdown of mica.

Above: Mudstones and distinctive Manly Beacon from Zabriskie Point.
Right: The subtle colors of Artists Palette.

Top: Eroded mudstone formations in Golden Canyon.

Right: A hiker is dwarfed by Natural Bridge.

Golden Canyon

I n the late afternoon light, this canyon's name is clearly justified. The yellow mudstones and siltstones take on a golden hue; they almost glow.

Like the terrain at Zabriskie Point, Golden Canyon has been uplifted and carved within the last few million years. Originally sediments including the forerunners of evaporite minerals such as borax and gypsum were deposited in flat, horizontal layers in shallow lakes. Later they were tilted as a result of faulting. The yellowish rocks are folded and tilted beds of ancient lakes that were deposited even before the creation of Lake Manly.

Because of its proximity to Furnace Creek, Golden Canyon is one of the most visited sites within Death Valley National Monument. The turnoff into the canyon is just three miles south of the visitor center. Red clay, used by the Panamint Indians for body paint, can be clearly seen on the lower slopes of the hillsides near the canyon entrance.

Mosaic Canyon

J ust southwest of Stovepipe Wells Village, at the end of an improved dirt road, one of the finest hikes within Death Valley National Monument begins. Mosaic Canyon enters Tucki Mountain from the north and immediately penetrates the water-polished white, gray, and black eroded fragments of rock that comprise a "mosaic." These rocks have been re-cemented together after having been broken apart, transported, and then buried at their present location millions of years ago. (The rocks were originally part of what geologists call the *Noonday Dolomite formation*, which is today the canyon's steep west wall.) A large fault later split the beds apart, forming a canyon along the split by the downcutting force of moving water. As one walks up the canyon, the "mosaics" floor is occasionally exposed through the coarse sand and gravel of the canyon bottom. Patches of pure white marble can also be observed on the canyon walls.

Above: Inviting Mosaic Canyon.

Inset top: The forces of nature break up rock and re-cement it into different patterns, seen here in Mosaic Canyon.

Inset bottom: Shattered carbonite in the walls of Fall Canyon.

*Arrow weed grows in
cornstalk-like formations in Death
Valley's Devils Cornfield.*

Devils Cornfield

Just southeast of Stovepipe Wells Village lies a curious arrangement of plants that, from a distance, appear like corn shocks. Actually they are clumps of arrow weed, *Pluchea sericea,* a member of the Sunflower Family. These perennials are widely distributed in Death Valley, wherever groundwater rises close to the surface. Wind erosion has removed the uppermost layers of soil, a process called deflation, except where the roots of the arrowweed have held it fast. Each clump reflects a point at which water is close enough to the surface to support the arrowweed.

Salt Creek and Pupfish

About fifteen miles north of the Monument Visitor Center lies Salt Creek, a perennial stream existing in the hottest, driest place in North America! As its name implies, the water is salty, comparable to the salinity of ocean water. The salt deposits along the edge of the stream contain carbonate and sulfate but are mostly table salt. The water originates in the Mesquite Flat drainage basin, two miles north of historic Stovepipe Well, but does not flow on the surface until it reaches McLean Spring. Salt Creek is a result of rock layers which have been uplifted along faults, forcing ground water to the surface.

Not surprisingly, the water attracts a number of plants and animals that would not otherwise survive here. Certainly the most interesting animal is one species of pupfish, *Cyprinodon salinus,*

which is found nowhere else in the world. This species is considered a relic from a time thousands of years ago when Death Valley was part of a huge river and lake system that began in the Sierra Nevada to the west and ended in Death Valley. Pupfish were more widely distributed at that time, but as the region became more arid since the close of the Pleistocene Epoch 10,000 years ago, and the connecting rivers and the lakes vanished, this species has become endemic to Death Valley. Now it is totally isolated and confined to Salt Creek.

During the winter months the pupfish lie dormant in the mud at the bottom of the creek and are rarely seen. However, by March they are active again with males establishing underwater territories which they defend against intrusion by other males. Spawning has been known to occur as early as February and continue through summer in the deeper pools. Young pupfish reach maturity in two to three months, and several generations can be produced each year. Pupfish feed upon algae and tiny insects, crustaceans and snails which they may scoop from the bottom or, in moving water, capture while the prey drifts by.

Pupfish are among the most heat-tolerant fish known. They can stand temperatures of from 104 to 111°F and daily fluctuations in water temperature that involve changes spanning 36°. Some pupfish are also strikingly tolerant of high salinity levels, up to 3.7 times that of seawater.

Many other animals frequent the Salt Creek area, attracted by the water. Great blue herons, common snipes, spotted sandpipers and killdeers have all been seen along or in Salt Creek. Herons are known to capture and consume the pupfish here. Coyotes and kit foxes have also been seen in the vicinity. In earlier times Panamint Indians fished for pupfish, using large porous baskets to scoop them up. Piles of fish were then baked between layers of tule reeds and hot ashes.

Top: The Salt Creek area, one of the few places in Death Valley where running water, spring-fed, flows year-round.

Above: Pupfish at Cottonball Marsh.

Rock Art and Petroglyphs

Prehistoric humans in the Death Valley region have left evidence of their lives in the engravings and paintings preserved on rock surfaces. Engravings or "petroglyphs" are designs chipped or scored into the faces of rocks; they are much more abundant in Death Valley National Monument than are paintings or "pictographs." In Greenwater Canyon both forms of rock art can be found. Although much of the artwork consists of strange patterns and designs, numerous forms can be recognized including lizards, snakes, scorpions, deer, bighorn sheep and dancing humans.

Within Death Valley National Monument excellent examples of rock art can be seen in Echo Canyon, Cottonwood Canyon, and at Klare Spring in Titus Canyon. At many of these sites it is obvious that certain designs are older than others. Sometimes one figure may be drawn over another, or one design may be lighter in color and seem "fresher" than another. Because petroglyphs were scratched into the surface of the rock, the dark surface stains of iron and manganese oxides were removed, revealing the untainted rock beneath. "Desert varnish" stains accumulate with time and thus petroglyphs darken as they become older. Some of the rock art is thought to be thousands of years old, made by people of the so-called Mesquite Flat Culture who lived within Death Valley from approximately 3,000 B.C. until 1 A.D.

Top: A boulder covered with petroglyphs, chipped into the desert varnish.

Above, left: A bighorn drawing graces a boulder on Hunter Mountain.

Above, right: A variety of petroglyph designs.

Wildrose Charcoal Kilns

T he best preserved remains of Death Valley's early mining period are the Wildrose Charcoal Kilns. Standing twenty-five feet with an average diameter of approximately thirty-one feet, the ten perfectly aligned kilns are located in upper Wildrose Canyon in the Panamint Mountains.

The Swiss-designed kilns were constructed in 1877 by Chinese laborers. Native rocks, bound with mortar, were used as building stones. The beehive shape of the Wildrose Kilns was considered desirable for strength and efficiency in manufacturing charcoal, sorely needed to fire the smelters at the Modoc Mine in the Argus Mountains, just fifteen miles west of the kilns. This mine produced both lead and silver ore

from deposits discovered in 1875. Wildrose Canyon in the Panamint Mountains, where pinyon pines covered the mountainsides, was the closest, most accessible location where fuel was available for making charcoal. It is said that Panamint Indians were hired to cut the pinyon pine logs used in the kilns. It took a long work day to fill the kilns with pinyon logs and another fifteen days before the charcoal was ready to be transported the fifteen miles to the smelter at the Modoc Mine.

The Wildrose Charcoal Kilns operated for only two or three years, from 1877 to perhaps 1880. Improved smelting procedures abroad resulted in ores being shipped elsewhere to be refined and the last smelter in the Death Valley region had probably shut down by 1885. The kilns have been restored twice and thus appear much as they did when in operation.

Above: Wildrose charcoal kilns under a blanket of snow.

Death Valley Wildlife

From tiny desert shrews to majestic bighorn sheep, Death Valley National Monument harbors a surprising variety of animal life. Four hundred and forty-three vertebrate animals are known to breed within the Monument boundaries, including 4 kinds of toads, 36 reptile species, 346 species of birds, and 57 species of mammals. Included within this list are three species of pupfish found nowhere else in the world.

Certainly Death Valley's most picturesque animal is the bighorn sheep. A mature ram may reach 200 pounds and, with its muscular torso and massive curled horns, is the largest native animal within the Monument boundaries. Bighorns are partial to rocky mountainsides; a glimpse of one is usually reserved for the more ambitious hiker. About 500 make their home in the mountains of Death Valley National Monument. The cat-sized kit fox is occasionally seen scampering across roadways at night. These large-eared canines become active at dusk as they begin their nightly search for kangaroo rats and rabbits, their chief prey. Ringtails, bobcats, grey foxes and coyotes are among the larger predators within the Monument, but like bighorn and kit foxes, these animals are rarely seen.

Visitors most frequently encounter the smaller animals of Death Valley. The antelope ground squirrel, distinguished by striped sides and a tail that is conspicuously white underneath, is common in areas of coarse soil and rock. Jet black ravens are observed on most any day, usually as they glide overhead in search of food scraps at campgrounds or perhaps a jackrabbit carcass on the road. Roadrunners nest in the trees and shrubs surrounding Furnace Creek Ranch and other parts of the Monument where the insects and the ubiquitous side-blotched lizard are common. The latter reptile is charac-

terized by a two-inch body adorned with light stripes (female) or speckled with blue and yellow (male). Individuals can be seen basking on rocks on any calm day, even in winter when all other reptiles are in hibernation.

Although some visitors to Death Valley fear they must contend with venomous creatures such as rattlesnakes, scorpions, or centipedes, in truth these animals are rarely encountered. The vast majority of visitors never see any of the four species of rattlesnakes known to occur within the Monument boundaries. Scorpions are nocturnal and thus active when visitors are in their tents, campers or hotel rooms. (None of the scorpion species within Death Valley are considered dangerous.) In fact, the most unusual creature that visitors might encounter is the large spider known as the tarantula. Males are often seen in the fall months, searching for mates. Ferocious as they may appear, tarantulas are quite harmless.

The surprising diversity of animal life that exists within Death Valley National Monument is a testament to the superb behavioral adaptations these animals have made to their environment. Unlike plants that have no choice but to endure environmental extremes, animals are mobile and move into more favorable microenvironments when advantageous. Many desert animals are nocturnal, becoming active at night when temperatures are lower and the air more humid. Small animals such as pocket mice, kangaroo rats and ground squirrels, and even large animals, such as bobcats, burrow underground where temperatures may never rise above 80°F. White-crowned sparrows, western bluebirds and ruby-crowned kinglets spend only the mild winters in Death Valley. With the onset of warm weather they fly away to milder climates.

Top: A desert tortoise.
Center: Roadrunner.
Above: Desert hairy scorpion.

Above: A coyote at sunrise, after a night's hunt.
Far left: Tarantula.
Left, top: A side-blotched lizard.
Left, below: Kangaroo rat.

CHAPTER THREE

The Historic Period: Prospectors, Mines, and Castles

Few regions in the West are more closely linked with the burro-accompanied desert prospector than is Death Valley. Thousands came, most left, and a few stayed long enough to be buried in the land that never gave them the permanent wealth they sought. Shorty Harris, Cap Lemoigne, Seldom Seen Slim — all died penniless. Yet they spent their lives scouring the valley floor and surrounding mountains on the chance that they would strike it rich.

The history of mining and prospectors in the Death Valley region began with the ill-fated Jayhawker Party and their stories of the Lost Gunsight Mine. While struggling out of the valley in 1849, one of the Jayhawkers, an unknown Mississippian, by chance picked up a piece of silver ore while looking for the sight which had fallen off his gun. It is believed the ore came from a rock outcrop along Emigrant Wash, somewhere between the present-day Stovepipe Wells Village and Emigrant Ranger Station. That night, around the campfire, the Mississippian whittled a new gunsight from the silver in the rock. Short of food and water, neither he nor any of the Jayhawkers could afford to linger at the place of discovery and were forced to proceed towards Los Angeles. By the time they reached civilization, six weeks later, talk of the small silver fragment had mushroomed into tales of "a mountain of silver." Death Valley's first mining boom was born.

Numerous prospectors came in search of the Lost Gunsight Mine, including William Manly and Asahel Bennett of Forty-niner fame. They returned in 1862 but failed to locate the silver ore outcrop. In 1864 a party led by Darwin French also failed to locate the Gunsight but did

Opposite: The tramway towers and cables of the Keane Wonder Mine.

Above: A wheel from one of the borax wagons, pulled by the famed 20-Mule teams.

A prospector packing his mules.

position to ward off any law officers that might come searching for them. They only had to wait a few months until interest in their evil deed cooled down.

At some point during their exile in the Panamints, one of the bandits discovered a vein of silver ore — one so big that it made their stolen box of bullion seem pitifully insignificant. Not surprisingly, they were reluctant to leave their fortress and go into the nearest town to file the claim. Their only recourse was to try and square things with the Wells Fargo Company, but that would take some delicate negotiating. Luckily, or oddly depending upon one's point of view, one of the desperados knew Senator William M. Stewart of nearby Nevada, a tough politican known throughout the West and a great promoter of silver mining. One of the robbers was able to sneak away from the hideout and ask the Senator to act as a go-between with the Wells Fargo Company. Although the precise details vary from one account to the next, it seems that Senator Stewart, after eyeing the ore samples supplied by the bandit, got Wells Fargo to agree to a repayment settlement. In return, the Senator received a very large share in the mining interests of the robbers. With all parties in agreement, the robbers filed their claims and Panamint silver became the talk of the West. The rush to the Panamint Mountains was on.

Within a year, a city appeared complete with a newspaper, saloons, and plenty of dance-hall girls. Although its thousand or so inhabitants would not make Panamint City the biggest boom town ever to appear in the Death Valley region, the fortune-hunters it attracted certainly made it the toughest. Fearful that members of the town's criminal element might conspire to rob shipments of silver headed towards the railhead, one mine owner devised a plan that would thwart the boldest

find the old Antimony Mine above present-day Wildrose Ranger Station. This latter mine, discovered in the 1860's, was probably the earliest to operate in Death Valley. To this day the fate of the lost Gunsight mine remains a mystery.

The first real boom town to spring up in the Death Valley region was Panamint City. Located not in the desert, but high in the Panamint Mountains, its beginnings were unusual to say the least. In the winter of 1873, five bandits robbed a Wells Fargo stage and made off with an express box filled with silver bullion. They fled into the Panamint Mountains via Surprise Canyon. Well-stocked with provisions, they counted on their remote location and strategic

highwayman. Senator Stewart directed his mill boss to cast the silver into 700-pound cannon balls, to be loaded into freight wagons and shipped without guards. There was only one road out of the Panamints and no place for bandits to divert a cargo of such size. And robbers did not have the necessary means to melt down the huge silver balls into something more manageable. Not surprisingly, no holdups ever took place and the shipments arrived safely at their destination.

Panamint City was a boom town destined to become a ghost town. By the late 1870s the silver ore was becoming too difficult to extract. When the town and access road were wiped out by successive floods, most people packed up and headed for more fertile pickings.

The Twenty Mule Team Days

One of the most spectacular episodes in the history of the West took place during the five years that twenty-mule teams hauled borax out of Death Valley. Each team pulled two huge wagons loaded with ten tons of borax and a 1,200 gallon watertank — a total hauling weight of thirty-six tons. Their route began at Harmony Borax Works, one mile north of today's Furnace Creek Ranch. Their destination was the nearest railhead at the town of Mojave: ten days and 165 barren, rugged desert miles away.

Death Valley's borax story began in 1873 when the *Inyo Independent* newspaper announced that the compound had been discovered on the valley floor. But the initial claims were not developed until 1881, when Aaron Winters of nearby Ash Meadows, Nevada, sold his Death Valley claim for $20,000 to William T. Coleman of San Francisco. Coleman was an entrepreneur already involved in borax mining in Nevada. The strike, one mile north of Furnace Creek, became known as the Harmony Borax Works. Here Coleman's "Greenland Salt and Borax Company" erected several adobe and stone buildings, wooden warehouses, a boiler, and thirty-six huge crystallization tanks.

Several steps were necessary before the valuable "white stuff" was ready for industrial use. At the Harmony claim, borax appeared as soft white fluff around the marsh on the

Top: 20-Mule Team Canyon, named after (but not used by) the stalwart borax wagons. Portions of the film Return of the Jedi *were filmed here.*

Above: Borax was hauled in this huge wagon, now on display at Harmony Borax works.

Harmony Borax Works, site of borax processing in the 1880's. The value and utility of borax compounds has been known since ancient times. Marco Polo reputedly brought borax back from Mongolia, where the Chinese were known to have used it for over sixteen centuries in their porcelain glazes. Composed of sodium, oxygen, boron, and water molecules, borax forms white crystals; and is usually found in dry lake beds. In industry, borax is used to remove impurities from molten materials and as a flux in welding. It also makes an excellent cleansing agent, and is needed in the manufacture of many types of glass, enamel, and fertilizer. Recently, it has been put to use in nuclear reactor shields and in the production of fiberglass.

valley floor. The fluff was collected by Chinese laborers, placed in large baskets, and hauled to the Harmony refinery on sledges. At the refinery, borax was allowed to crystallize on iron rods suspended in large vats. Things went well during the winter of 1883-1884, but the refining process failed during the summer months when high temperatures prevented the borax from crystallizing. Coleman's company overcame the problem by moving the operation close to the town of Shoshone, near another source of borax, during the summer months. Less than fifty miles as the crow flies from Furnace Creek, Shoshone had cooler summer temperatures due to its higher elevation. The last and most serious obstacle to the commercial success of Coleman's "Greenland Salt and Borax Company" was getting the refined borax to market. The closest railhead — at Mojave — was separated from the Harmony Borax Works by miles of rocky desert.

Coleman's solution involved the use of durable mules — several teams of them — to pull giant wagons through the desert. The enormous hauling wagons were constructed soley for the Death Valley borax shipments. Probably the largest wagons ever used, each could carry a ten-ton payload. The rear wheels stood seven feet high and were protected with steel tires eight inches wide and an inch thick. The wagon beds stretched sixteen feet, were four feet wide with sides six feet high. Empty, each wagon weighed 7,800 pounds. It is not clear who designed them but historian L. Burr Belden believes that at least some of them were built in San Bernardino by the Bright and Chute Wagon Works for a cost of about $900 apiece. Considering the difficulty of the terrain over which they traveled, the wagons were remarkably free of breakdowns during the five years they were in use. Only the steel tires had to be replaced with any regularity.

The road to Mojave traversed 165 miles of treacherous desert. Waterholes were fifty miles apart with dusty, rocky, sandy ruts serving for roads in between. Teams traveled from fifteen to seventeen miles a day, resulting in a journey of ten days between the Harmony Borax Works and the Mojave railhead. Two men rode the wagons: the driver and his assistant, called a "swamper." Generally speaking the teamsters were men of few words, were without wives or children, and were considered reliable employees who could be trusted with the $10,000 to $15,000 worth of property under their supervision. Journalist John Spears, writing in 1892, described the mule-driver's occupation: "The life of a teamster on the desert is not only one of hardship, it is in places extremely dangerous. There are grades, like the one on the road from Granite Spring to Mojave, where the plunge is steep, the roadbed as hard as a turnpike. The load must go down, so when the brink is reached, the driver throws his weight on the brake of the front wagon, the swamper handles the brake on the rear, and away they go, creaking, groaning and gliding, until the bottom is reached."

From 1883 to 1888, the twenty-mule teams delivered their loads to Mojave with surprising precision, considering the difficulty of the terrain and the scorching summertime temperatures. It was a reasonably profitable venture for Coleman and no doubt would have remained that way were it not for Coleman's poor investments in other enterprises, the discovery of borax deposits closer to the rail lines, and the development of new processing technology. Much later, the romance and adventure spurred by the long haul of the twenty mule teams from Death Valley would become an advertising symbol for the U.S. Borax Company and the popular radio and television show "Death Valley Days" which it sponsored.

Greenwater and Copper Mining

"Here today and gone tomorrow" best describes Greenwater. In 1906 the town's total population was seventy. In just one month it had jumped to one thousand with over 2,500 mining claims staked out in the surrounding hills. Greenwater would be promoted as "The Greatest Copper Camp on Earth," yet by December of 1907 — just over one year later — the town was abandoned.

The stampede began in 1906 as a result of a prospector's discovery and claim filing for a mineral deposit located along the eastern slopes of the Black Mountains. The mineral was not gold, silver or even borax, but a greenish ore containing copper. Rumors were rampant about the extent of the deposits. Some enthusiasts claimed the ground was 75% copper for seventy square miles!

The news traveled like wildfire and investors popped up everywhere. There seemed no shortage of investment capital, with as much as $200,000 being paid for those claims that were staked first. Stock was made available in New York with shares going for up to $250 each. Arthur Kunze, the prospector who filed first, received $150,000 for his claim, much of it stock in a syndicate that would become known as the Greenwater Copper Mine and Smelter Company.

There was just one problem with mining copper in the Greenwater district — there were only a few small, subsurface deposits. As the miners discovered after just a few months, the veins went "neither down, up, nor sideways." When the news got out that Greenwater copper simply wasn't materializing as hoped, money vanished overnight, stock became worthless, and almost every newspaper office, bank, boarding house, and store was vacated within thirty days. In short, Greenwater became the example of the get-rich-quick schemes so prevalent among the eastern businessmen who looked to the West for their fortune.

Gold Mines

Two of the most important gold mining areas within Death Valley National Monument were located around the town of Skidoo and at the Keane Wonder Mine.

Lying just north of Emigrant Pass, the mines surrounding Skidoo held the

Left: An old mill, a dangerously unstable but historic site.

Top: Old cans and debris are all that remain at the ghost town of Greenwater.

Above: Early newspapers encouraged miners and opportunists to come to Greenwater.

Above: Desert vegetation in Fall Canyon.

Right: Beavertail prickly pear cactus.

ing the murder. It seems a drunken saloon keeper named Joe Simpson shot the town banker dead. The law-abiding citizens promptly hanged Simpson and buried him on Boot Hill. Unfortunately, it took several days for a Herald reporter covering the story to arrive from Los Angeles: he missed the hanging by just twenty-four hours. The townsfolk, honored by the presence of a big city reporter and eager not to disappoint him, promptly dug up Simpson and hanged him again. The reporter got his photographs and the seven hundred residents of Skidoo had their town name appear in print across the country.

The Keane Wonder Mine was another gold producer, located in the Funeral Mountains on the opposite side of Death Valley from Skidoo. Discovered in 1903 by Jack Keane and Domingo Atcheson, its ore samples were impressive enough to sell the mine for $150,000 even before any digging began. The investment paid off and by 1907 a twenty-stamp mill was in operation crushing 1,800 tons of ore each month. The mill's unique tramway system was constructed to use the weight of the ore coming down to generate power for the crushers. Today, a high clearance road leads visitors to the old mill foundation and a rusting bullwheel, all that remain of the operation. A one-mile trail leads up the mountainside to the mine.

relatively unusual distinction of having made money for their owners. Between 1905 and 1917 nearly six million dollars in gold was extracted at a cost of about three million. Such profits explained why both telephone and stage service existed at Skidoo, luxuries few other boom towns possessed. What Skidoo didn't have when it was founded was water. No spring existed near the mines, so water had to be piped in from Telescope Peak, 23 miles distant. Born from this project was the then-popular slang expression "twenty-three skidoo," a cute way of saying scram.

Although Skidoo was peaceful by mining town standards, it became famous for a sensational murder, or rather the peculiar publicity surround-

"Heroes of Death Valley"
The Civilian Conservation Corps

The Civilian Conservation Corps, established in 1933 by President Franklin Delano Roosevelt, helped provide jobs during the Great Depression. Men working on CCC project crews were paid $25.00 a month: $20.00 sent directly to his family and $5.00 paid to the worker for his personal expenses.

In October of 1933, shortly after Death Valley was established as a National Monument, CCC companies 539 and 530, from Kentucky and Ohio respectively, arrived to help in establishing this remote, arid area as a winter haven for tourists. After a short time spent in tents at Furnace Creek Ranch, the two companies were moved to Cow Creek. Within two weeks, the twin camps of Cow Creek and Funeral Range were built, everyone housed and the mess halls in operation — and the work began. Roads, entry stations, spring development and campgrounds were some of the projects accomplished by CCC crews.

Companies 530 and 539 left in the spring of 1934, before the excessive summer heat began. In October of that year companies 1240 and 1246 from New York and New Jersey moved into

camps Cow Creek and Funeral Range. The project work continued. In addition, a CCC camp was established at a higher elevation at Wildrose. Company 908 from California spent the summer of 1935 continuing trail and road work there. That fall they moved to Cow Creek and were joined by California company 904.

During their first three years in Death Valley, the CCC built 343 miles of new road, developed 12 springs, and established five campgrounds. Three ranger stations and checking booths were erected. The Park Village was laid out and comfortable residences complete with driveways and landscaping constructed.

CCC companies continued to work in Death Valley until 1942, when World War II brought about a national change in economic and personal conditions. The CCC was then disbanded, but not before these hardworking men had completely transformed remote Death Valley into an accessible National Monument. Their efforts in building, maintaining and manning the new Monument's numerous facilities made it possible for the American public to visit and enjoy this unique area.

Above: Civilian Conservation Corps workers.

Above right: Death Valley Scotty and companion at the Castle gates.

Above left: Scotty and Albert Johnson remember earlier glory days of train travel — and speed records.

Death Valley Scotty

Death Valley's most famous prospector probably never made a nickel from a mine or vein of precious metal. But for decades he was thought to be the wealthiest man ever to strike it rich in the Death Valley region and, in many respects, he did just that. His real name was Walter E. Scott but became known to millions as Death Valley Scotty.

Born on September 20, 1872, Walter Scott was a native Kentuckian. The youngest of six children, he was destined to claim more notoriety than any of his siblings. His father bred and trained trotting horses and Scotty was raised to be comfortable and confident in the saddle. While still a boy, Walter traveled out West to join two of his older brothers and take on the life of a cowhand. The brothers ended up not far from Death Valley, at Humboldt Wells, Nevada. According to Scotty, he was not yet fifteen when he got a job as a

swamper on one of the famed twenty-mule team wagons out of the Harmony Borax Works. Just how long he stayed with the Coleman Company is not known but in 1890 he was "discovered" by a talent scout from the Buffalo Bill Wild West Show. He accepted a job as a roper, shooter and trick rider.

For the next eleven years Scotty traveled throughout the U.S. and Europe as part of Buffalo Bill's show. He loved the spotlight, and although he never became one of the show's headliners, his experiences at this point in his career influenced the rest of his life. He would never be content as a spectator.

Scotty stayed with the Wild West Show until he had a disagreement with his employer, Buffalo Bill. Although Scotty's career as a trick rider was over, another more profitable career was about to begin. Through contacts he had made while with the Wild West Show he was able to gain an appointment with a Mr. Julian Gerard, a wealthy businessman from New York. Scotty carried two gold nuggets when he arrived at Gerard's office in 1902. He convinced Gerard that they were from a gold mine Scotty had discovered: if Gerard would grubstake him, the gold mine could be relocated and mined, bringing in a fortune for both of them. Gerard was no fool, but one must consider the climate of the times. To an Easterner, the West was a land of exploration and excitement. Scotty offered a piece of this excitement — and the possibility of a tremendous return — for a relatively small investment.

Scotty used Gerard's $10,000 to assemble the best pack outfits money could buy. But he did not spend much time digging for gold. According to a Daggett storekeeper "he spent far more time in the saloons than he did on the desert." Los Angeles newspaper accounts from that time tell of a "W. Scott of Death Valley who paid for everything with $100 bills and was renowned for his generous tipping of bellboys and chambermaids while staying at the best hotels the city had to offer." When Scotty returned to New York and told Gerard that he was not able to relocate the mine which had held so much promise, Gerard was left with "nothing to show for it but a pile of correspondence and two gold nuggets."

When Gerard's money-well closed Scotty was left without a sponsor. But not for long. In 1904, Scotty met Albert M. Johnson, an insurance executive from Chicago. Johnson and Scotty were opposites in almost every way. Scotty was gregarious and loud; Johnson was shy and retiring. Scotty was a man of floating morals often prone to activities that would cause him trouble with the law; Johnson was deeply religious and an outstanding citizen. But the most important difference between the two men was that Scotty, regardless of his claims to the contrary, was usually broke and in debt; Johnson was a millionaire with vast holdings in a number

of successful enterprises. Strangely, the two would become lifelong companions. Johnson became the only gold mine Scotty would ever know.

Some say that Albert Johnson lived out his boyhood fantasies through Walter E. Scott; that Scotty was Johnson's entertainment. Whatever the reason for their friendship, it endured for over forty years. In October of 1904, Scotty struck a deal with Johnson and his partner, Edward A. Shedd. The latter two men would receive two thirds of any mining properties or claims and Scotty would get what was left over. In turn Scotty would be grubstaked to the tune of $2,500 and would proceed immediately to the Death Valley region to get his mine operational. But Scotty had other ideas. After stopping briefly in Goldfield, Nevada, he headed, once again, to Los Angeles and embarked upon a wild spending spree that got Scotty much publicity and resulted in Edward Shedd giving up any hopes of a return on his money. However, Johnson's interest in Scotty's gold mine remained and in 1905 he became a partner in Scotty's prospecting ventures.

Scotty's fortunes were certainly on the upswing, culminating in his most famous exploit — the record-breaking train ride from Los Angeles to Chicago. Quietly backed by E. Burdon Gaylord, a Los Angeles businessman, and the Santa Fe Railroad, Scotty announced that he had hired his own special train to cover the distance between the two cities faster than anyone had ever done before. The news media of the day gobbled up the story. Before the train departed on July 9, 1905, Scotty's exploit made newspaper headlines from coast to coast. On July 11 the train arrived in Chicago, having covered the 2,265-mile route in just under 45 hours. The record was broken, the public was ecstatic, and Walter Scott was a national hero whose

Albert and Bessie Johnston

Top: The Upper Music Room at Scottys Castle.

Lower: A spiral staircase leads down from the Music Room.

Opposite: Scottys Castle on a rainy winter day.

Inset: A prospector-and-mule weathervane atop the birdwatching tower.

name was on the lips of millions of Americans for months to come.

In the early 1900s Albert Johnson made numerous trips into the Death Valley region with Scotty acting as guide and trail boss, a job no one could do as well as Walter E. Scott. One must remember that Scotty was an excellent horseman and knew the Death Valley region as well as anyone. With his campfire stories of mines and prospectors it is hard to imagine anyone being better entertainment than Scotty.

Even though the mine was never found, Johnson became increasingly attached to the desert environment. By 1915 he had decided to spend a portion of each winter in Death Valley. His wife said she would accompany him on the condition that a proper home be constructed, suitable for entertaining the friends and relatives who might visit. Scotty would help find the site. Johnson began buying up land around Death Valley's northern boundaries with an eye on building a permanent residence. Construction on Johnson's "Death Valley Ranch" began in 1922. Although the house was not planned to be a castle, it had reached that stature by 1931 when the great depression brought all work to a halt.

All during the construction period, Scotty was highly visible, referring to the building as "my castle." Johnson stayed in the background and seemed quite pleased not to have the press clamoring at his heels. The building soon became known as "Scottys Castle," and Johnson seemed quite content to leave it that way.

The Moorish style house is indeed an impressive structure, especially considering its remote location. In the early construction phase, money was no object for the multimillionaire Johnson. The castle interior was adorned with imported and hand-carved furniture; European artwork hung on every wall. A custom-made theater organ was

moved into the music room, and the castle was outfitted with solar water heating and its own diesel generator to provide electricity. When work stopped in 1931, the castle contained over 31,000 square feet of floor space with stables, guest houses, and a 56-foot chimes tower.

The depression was rough on Johnson's finances and he was forced to halt construction of the castle. He could no longer afford to complete the castle's huge swimming pool (it still stands empty today) or finish the terraced landscaping that had originally been planned. Rather than attempt to rebuild his empire, he elected to retire and move out West. His last two residences were a home in the Hollywood Hills near Los Angeles, and of course his "castle" in Death Valley.

Johnson and Scotty remained friends throughout their retirement years, with Scotty keeping busy entertaining the hundreds of people that came each winter to visit the castle. Albert Johnson died in 1948 but strangely did not leave the castle to Scotty. Death Valley Ranch was turned over to the Gospel Foundation of California, which Johnson had established. The Foundation did, however, allow Scotty to live on the premises and entertain the guests for the rest of his life. Scotty died in 1954 at the age of 82. He is buried on Windy Point, a hill overlooking the castle.

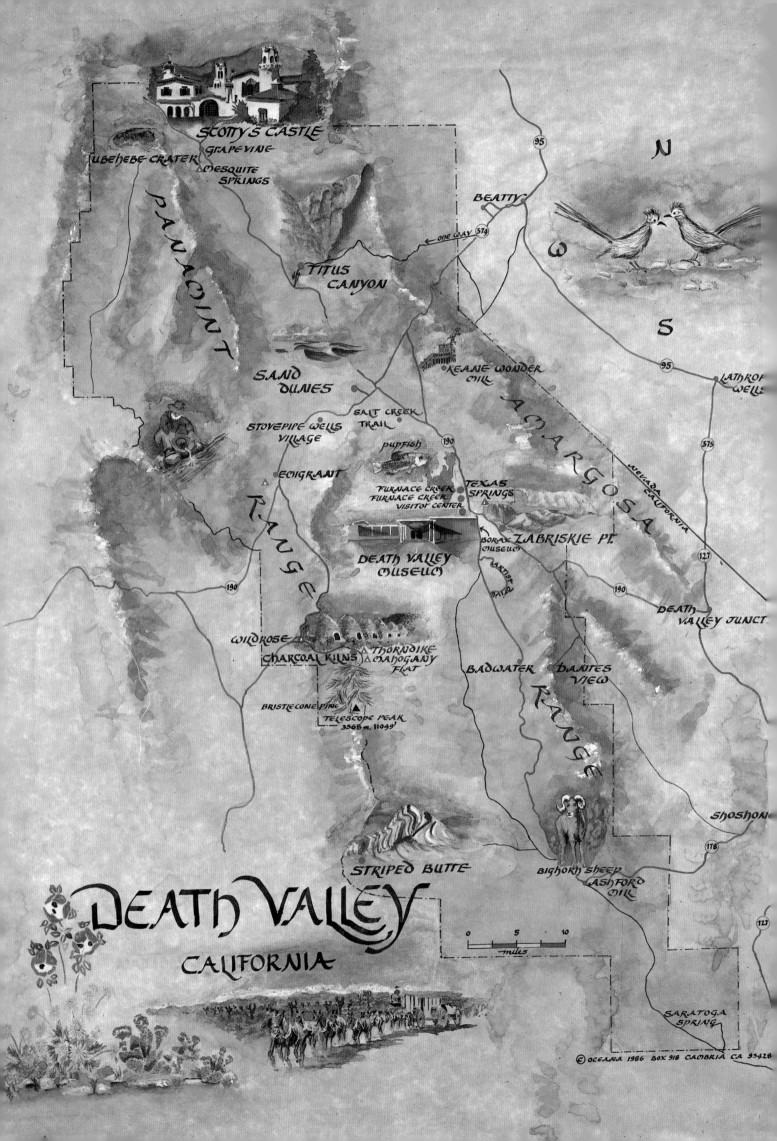

DEATH VALLEY
CALIFORNIA

SCOTTY'S CASTLE
GRAPEVINE
UBEHEBE CRATER
MESQUITE SPRINGS

PANAMINT

TITUS CANYON

BEATTY
ONE WAY 374
95

N
W E
S

95
LATHROP WELLS

SAND DUNES

KEANE WONDER MILL

AMARGOSA

SALT CREEK TRAIL

STOVEPIPE WELLS VILLAGE

PUPFISH

190

375

NEVADA / CALIFORNIA

EMIGRANT

FURNACE CREEK
FURNACE CREEK VISITOR CENTER

TEXAS SPRINGS

RANGE

BORAX MUSEUM

ZABRISKIE PT.

127

DEATH VALLEY MUSEUM

ARTIST DRIVE

190

DEATH VALLEY JUNCT.

WILDROSE
CHARCOAL KILNS

THORNDIKE
MAHOGANY FLAT

BADWATER

DANTES VIEW

RANGE

BRISTLECONE PINE
TELESCOPE PEAK
3368 m. 11049'

SHOSHONE

178

STRIPED BUTTE

BIGHORN SHEEP
ASHFORD MILL

127

0   5   10
miles

SARATOGA SPRING

© OCEANA 1986 BOX 918 CAMBRIA CA 93428